Who Are You Calling Junior?

To ETHAN & EMMA

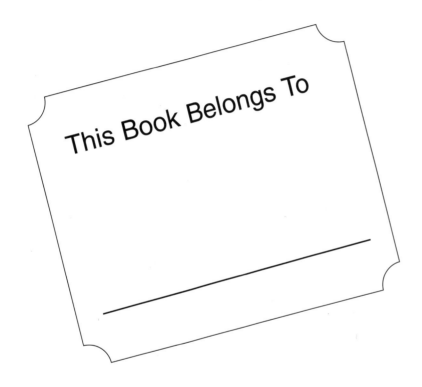

This Book Belongs To

_____

Visit Michael's website at
www.michaelfinklea.net

Who Are You Calling Junior?

Written by
Michael Finklea

Illustrated by
Russ Petty

Ozark Publishing • P.O. Box 228 • Prairie Grove, Arkansas 72753
800-371-7709

Library of Congress cataloging-in-publication data

Finklea, Michael, 1962-
        Who are you calling junior? / written by Michael Finklea ; illustrated by Russ Petty.
            p.   cm.
        Summary: Rhyming text provides clues about the habitat, behavior, and appearance of
an animal, which is revealed to be the Australian sugar glider. Includes a note with
additional facts about this tree-dwelling marsupial.
        ISBN 1-56763-420-6. -- ISBN 1-56763-421-4 (pbk.)
        1. Sugar glider--Juvenile literature. [1. Sugar glider.]   I. Sanders, Scott, ill. . II. Title.
QI737.M373F55 1998
.599.2'3--DC21   98-7459
                                                                                                          CIP
                                                                                                          AC

Inspired by

all the hours of fun I had playing with this special animal.
And, for all of the times I would call out his name,
and he would look at me, out of the corner of his eye,
as if to say "Who are you calling Junior?"

Hello, Mate.
What is your name?
My name is Junior.
Let's play a game.

I'll give you clues
As to what I am.
I just gave you one
From a foreign land!

Have you heard of me?
I'm far from new,
But I can't be found
At your local zoo.

I am the cutest little thing
That you ever did see.
There are two clues here.
Another—I live in the trees.

Now I sleep all day
And I am up all night.
Do I like the dark?
Or am I scared of light?

I am very small
So hold out your hand.
You could toss me up,
But where would I land?

I have great big eyes
And a long furry tail,
A soft coat of silk,
And gliding membranes to sail!

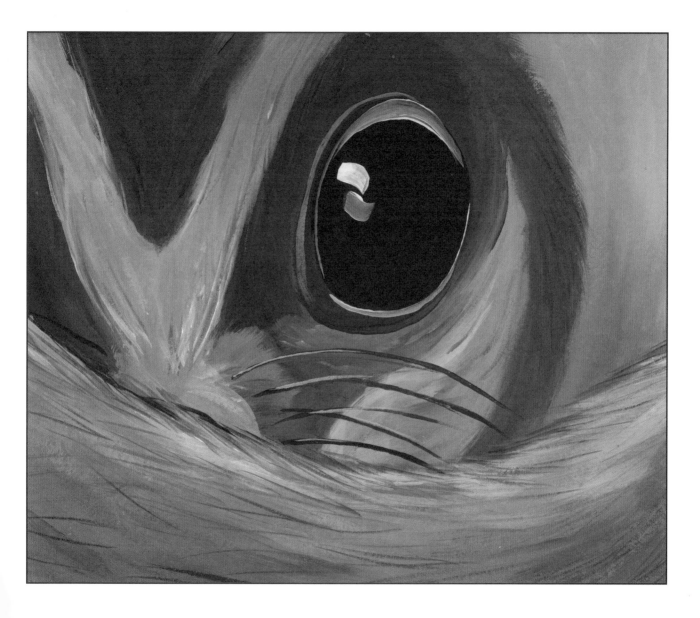

By now you may know
That I like to fly.
Can you guess by the puzzle?
Would you like to try?

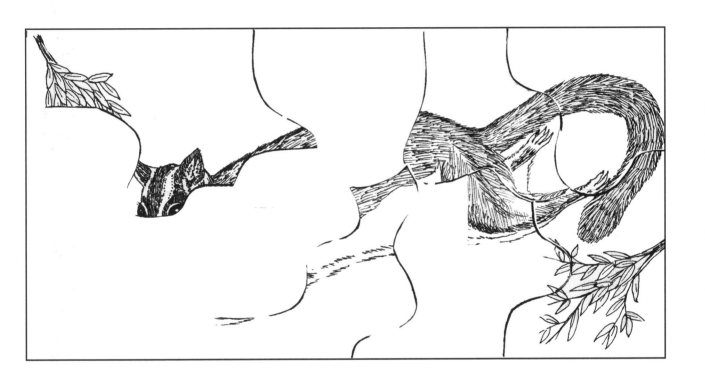

I cannot fly far.
I can only glide.
So I am not a bird,
But that was a good try.

If you're still not sure
How I get my name,
I love sweet sap
But veggies do the same.

The last clues are
I have to bond with you
Out of my mother's pouch
Like a kangaroo.

Junior is my name.
Did you like this game?
I'm sorry to keep you guessing.
Now I feel ashamed.

Read about me further
On the page to come.
I hope you had fun.
Now I have got to run!

Sugar gliders make great pets!

Sugar gliders are tiny tree-dwelling marsupials. A marsupial is a mammal that carries its young in an external pouch on the abdomen. They are true pouched animals in the same order as kangaroos and koalas.

These special animals are originally from Australia, Indonesia, and New Guinea. At adulthood their body is about five to six inches in length with about a six to seven-inch tail and weighs only five or six ounces.

The life expectancy of a glider is about seven to ten years. These little animals have been pets in Europe and their native lands for quite some time.

Sugar gliders get their name from their love of sweet sap and their gliding membrane which stretches from their wrist to their ankles. In the wild they cut notches in the Eucalyptus tree bark and lick up the sweet sap. The gliding membrane enables the sugar glider to travel from tree to tree. The glider uses its tail in flight for steering and also for carrying nesting materials.

The health and well-being of a sugar glider will depend on how much it is handled. A sugar glider needs to be handled three to four hours a day!

Special thanks to Bugsies Buddies, Vernon, Texas.
This was where I was first introduced to sugar gliders.
The information above was taken from a handout that was given to me to insure the best care for my new best friend.

About the Author . . .

Michael Finklea has written stories for the past seventeen years. *"Who Are You Calling Junior"* was the second book he wrote. At the end of May, 2005, it was estimated that Michael has spoken to over 2,000 elementary schools!

Now living in Charlotte, North Carolina, Michael will begin his eighth year of author visits. Please visit his website to see his other seven titles at www.michaelfinklea.net!

About the Artist . . .

Russ Petty has been painting professionally since 1995, but he has always had a love for art, even as a young boy, growing up in Spartanburg, South Carolina. He attended Francis Marion University in Florence, SC where he earned a bachelor's degree in Fine Arts.

Now, Mr. Petty lives in Pineville, North Carolina. His wife is an art teacher at a local middle School. They have a daughter named Mya. Do you think Mya will grow up to become an artist, too?